Being a Goalie

Andy Croft

Published in association with The Basic Skills Agency

Hodder & Stoughton

A MEMBER OF THE HODDER HEADLINE GROUP

Acknowledgements

Cover: Stu Forster/Allsport.

Photos: pp. 2, 9 © Allsport; p. 5 Empics Sports Photo Agency; pp. 11, 13, 15, 19, 23 © Action-Plus Photographic.

Orders: please contact Bookpoint Ltd, 39 Milton Park, Abingdon, Oxon OX14 4TD. Telephone: (44) 01235 827720 , Fax: (44) 01235 400454. Lines are open from 9.00-6.00, Monday to Saturday, with a 24 hour message answering service.   You can also order through our website, www.hodderheadline.co.uk

British Library Cataloguing in Publication Data
A catalogue record for this title is available from The British Library

ISBN 0 340 74721 8

First published 1999
Impression number   10 9 8 7 6 5 4
Year   2006   2005   2004

Typeset by Fakenham Photosetting Ltd, Fakenham, Norfolk.
Printed in Great Britain for Hodder & Stoughton Educational, a division of Hodder Headline, 338 Euston Road, London NW1 3BH by CPI Bath

Contents

1 The Most Important Player on the Pitch

It's hard being a goalie.

Strikers get all the credit when you win.
But the keeper gets the blame when you lose.
No one remembers your saves.
But everyone remembers your mistakes.

A good keeper is worth a goal
before the game starts.
A good keeper makes the rest of the team
feel confident.
A good keeper can make up for a bad defence.

But a bad keeper can lose a match.

A goalie's job is a hard one.

2   Goals!

Goals used to come in all shapes and sizes.
They didn't always have cross-bars.
In ancient China, goals were 30 feet high
and three feet wide!
The cross-bar was only invented in 1882.
Today the goal is eight yards wide
and eight feet high.

The goalkeeper used to be called
the 'net minder'.
He used to be allowed to handle the ball
outside the box.

There have been lots of famous goalkeepers.
Pope John Paul II used to play in goal.

Gordon Banks, Peter Shilton and David Seaman
have kept goal for England.
Neville Southall for Wales.
Jim Leighton for Scotland.
Pat Jennings for Northern Ireland.

Goalkeepers are often colourful characters.
Sheffield United once had a keeper
called Fatty Foulke.
He weighed 23 stone.
He liked to get up early before a game
just so he could eat the team's breakfast.
He once picked up a striker
and threw him into the goal.
Howard Barker was a famous amateur keeper.
He could really jump.
He was also the British high jump champion.

South American keepers like taking risks.
Chilavert is the Paraguay keeper.
He likes to run up the other end of the pitch
to help his team take corners.
Mexico once had a keeper called Campos.
He started a World Cup game in goal.
Then he played up front in the second half.
Higuita from Colombia
invented a new kind of save.
He called it the scorpion kick.

Higuita invented the scorpion kick.

Goalkeepers are often superstitious.
Derby County once had a keeper
called Jack Robinson.
He ate a bowl of rice pudding
before every game.
Just for luck.

The Russian keeper, Lev Yashin,
always had two caps.
He wore one.
He put the other in the goal.
Just for luck.

Manchester United keeper, Peter Schmeichel,
has three kits for every game.
He wears one during the warm-up.
Another in the first half.
And then he changes again at half-time.
Just for luck.

3　Lee

Lee isn't a famous keeper yet.
But he hopes to be famous one day.
He is certainly good enough.
He plays in his local under-15 league.
His team are not very good.
They only scored 13 goals last season.
But they didn't let in many goals.
Thanks to Lee.
They just avoided relegation.
Thanks to Lee.
He even saved a penalty in their last match.
His team mates voted him Player of the Year.
His favourite player is David Seaman.

Lee practises all the time.
He keeps fit.
And he thinks.
He thinks a lot about the keeper's job.

4   The Goalie's Job

Goalies don't have much to do.
They aren't expected to score.
They don't have to run very fast.
They never head the ball.
And they *never* dribble.
All goalkeepers have to do
is stop the ball going in the net.
They are even allowed to use their *hands*.
They only touch the ball
for a few minutes in a game.
In a good game they won't touch the ball at all.
Sounds easy, doesn't it?

Not when you play behind a shaky defence.
Like Lee.

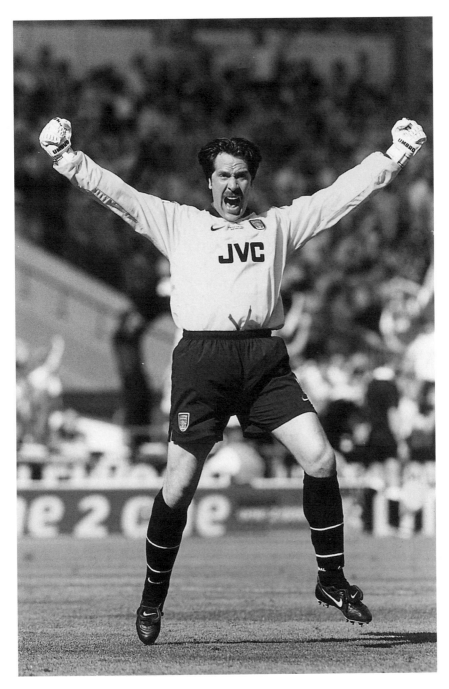

David Seaman celebrates.

5 Movement

A good keeper never stops moving.
He is always ready.
He stands on the edge of the six-yard box.
In the middle of the goal.
His feet apart.
His weight forward on the soles of his feet.
His head forward.
His hands ready.

When the ball moves to his right,
he skips sideways to the right.
When the ball moves to his left,
he skips sideways to the left.
He never stands still.
He always knows where his goal is.
He doesn't have to look behind him.

And he never stops talking.
He talks to his defenders.

Lee praises his defenders
when they play well.
But you should hear him shouting
if they make a mistake.

A good keeper is always ready.

6 Crosses

When a cross comes in
the keeper doesn't wait for it to reach him.
He attacks it.
He shouts for it.
He tries to catch it
at the highest point of the cross.
If he can't catch it he punches it away.
If the ball is coming from left or right
he uses one fist.
If the ball is coming straight at him
he uses two fists.
If he can't reach the ball
he stays on his line.

Not many crosses get past Lee.

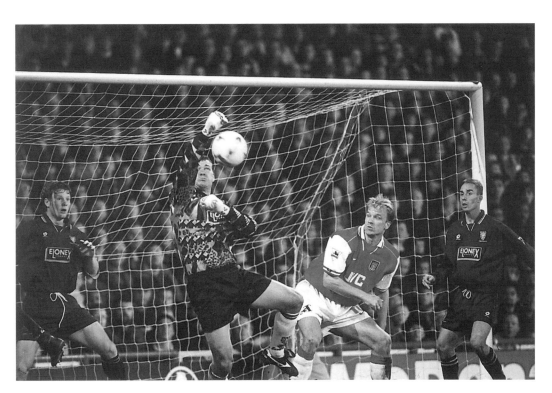

A keeper uses his hands.

7   Set-Pieces

The keeper is in charge for corners
and free kicks.
He shouts instructions to his defenders.
He keeps an eye on the ball.
He watches for players running into the box.

The keeper puts a defender
on each post for corners.
He stands in the middle of the goal line,
facing the ball.
If it is an inswinging corner
he's ready to catch it.
If it is an outswinging corner
he's ready to attack it.

For direct free kicks
the keeper arranges the wall.
The wall is made up of defenders.
They create a 'human' wall
to stop the ball going in the goal.
The wall covers one half of the goal.
The keeper covers the other half.
He must be able to see the ball at all times.

Teams don't score many set-pieces against Lee.

An Arsenal wall.

8   Shots

The best saves don't always look good.
But it is better to be safe than sorry.

Watch the ball at all times.
Get your body behind the shot.

If the shot is at ground level,
keep your feet together.
You might have to clear it with your feet.
But it is best to use your hands.
Kneel sideways.
One hand behind the ball.
The other hand above it.
Then gather the ball into your body.

Some shots are chest high.
With these you should trap the ball
between your hands, chest and chin.

If it is a high shot
you have to be ready to jump.
As fast and as high as you can.
Spread your fingers wide.

If you can't catch the ball,
deflect it round the post.

Lee knows it is better to give away a corner
rather than a goal.

9 Only the Keeper to Beat

The goalie is also the last defender.
The last man.

Don't come off your line too soon.
An attacker may chip the ball past you.
Or he might take the ball round you.

Run out of goal to narrow the angle.
Try to push the player wide.
But it is a risk.
You must win the ball.
It's an open goal if you don't win it.

But Lee usually does.

David Seaman jumps for a ball.

10   Distribution

When you hold the ball,
don't just get rid of it.
Hold onto it.
This gives your team
time to get their breath back.
And time to move up the pitch.
Then you can release it.

You can try a volley:
throw the ball up
and kick it in mid-air.
Or a half-volley:
throw the ball up and kick it
as it hits the ground.
You can throw it over-arm.
Or roll it under-arm.

Lee always tries to make sure
it goes to one of his own players.

11   Penalties

A penalty is like a duel
between two players.
It's a battle of wits.
It's a trial of skill.
It's also a matter of luck.

Don't be afraid.
No one really expects a goalkeeper
to save a penalty.
All the pressure is on the striker.
Everyone expects him to score.

Stare hard at the penalty-taker.
This shows you are not afraid.

Penalty-takers pick their spot
before they shoot.
Watch their eyes.

Right-footed players often put the ball
to your right.
Left-footed players often put the ball
to your left.

Most penalties are hit low.
Get down early and dive.
If you are unlucky
you will dive the wrong way.
But if you are lucky you will be a hero.

Like David Seaman.
Like Lee.

Diving to save a penalty.

12   Who Knows?

Lee hopes to be a professional
goalkeeper one day.
Like his hero David Seaman.
One day perhaps he will.
If he trains hard.
If he practises.
If he is lucky.

But Lee has other things
to worry about just now.
He recently hurt his hand.
He has been out of action for a few weeks.
His team are back in relegation trouble.
Last week they lost 10–16.
Lee will soon be back in goal.

He knows how to save goals.
But can he save his team?

If you have enjoyed reading this book, you may be
interested in other titles in the *Livewire
Investigates* series.

Basketball
Being an Actor
Being a Model
Being a Striker
Boxing
Bungee Jumping
Climbing the World's Highest Mountains
Hang Gliding
The Last Great Race on Earth
Motocross
Running with the Bulls
Skiing the Impossible
Stunt Flying
Surfing and Snowboarding
White Water Thrills
The World Cup